The ANCIENT MAYA

MYTHS of the WORLD

THE ANCIENT MAYA

VIRGINIA SCHOMP

MARSHALL CAVENDISH · BENCHMARK
NEW YORK

~ *For MFN Nicole Schomp* ~

The author would like to thank Robert J. Sharer,
Shoemaker Professor of Anthropology, University of Pennsylvania,
for his valuable comments and careful reading of the manuscript.

Benchmark Books Marshall Cavendish   99 White Plains Road   Tarrytown, New York 10591
www.marshallcavendish.us Text copyright ©2010 by Marshall Cavendish Corporation Map copyright © 2010 by Mike
Reagan. All rights reserved. No part of this book may be reproduced or utilized in any form or by any means electronic or
mechanical, including photocopying, recording, or by any information storage and retrieval system, without permission
from the copyright holders. All Internet sites were available and accurate when this book was sent to press. LIBRARY OF CON-
GRESS CATALOGING-IN-PUBLICATION DATA: Schomp, Virginia. The ancient Maya / by Virginia Schomp. p. cm. — (Myths of the
world) Summary: "A retelling of several important ancient Maya myths, with background information describing the history, geography, belief systems, and customs of the people" — Provided by the publisher. Includes bibliographical refer-
ences and index. ISBN 978-0-7614-4217-2 1. Maya mythology — Juvenile literature. 2. Maya cosmology — Juvenile
literature. I. Title. F1435.3.R3S36 2010 299.7'842013 — dc22 2008034956

EDITOR: Joyce Stanton   ART DIRECTOR: Anahid Hamparian
PUBLISHER: Michelle Bisson   SERIES DESIGNER: Michael Nelson
PHOTO RESEARCH : Connie Gardner   MAP: Mike Reagan

Cover photo by Banco del Atlantida Tegucigaipa/The Art Archive The photographs in this book are used by permission
and through the courtesy of: Art Archive: National Anthropological Museum Mexico, 1; Archaeological and Ethnological
Museum, Guatemala City, 10-11; Banco del Tegucigaipa, 21; SuperStock: age footstock, 93; Christie's Images, 28-29; The
Image Works: © SSPL, 50, 53; Mary Evans Picture Library, 74; © British Museum/Werner Forman Archive/Topham, 80,
85; Corbis: Charles and Josetta Lenars, 7-8; Michele Westmorland, 18; Kimball Art Museum, 19; Atlantide Phototravel,
69, 70; Smithsonian Institution, 70; The Granger Collection: 32; Alamy: Robert Harding Picture Library, 34 (B); Zach
Holmes, 46; Mireille Vautier, 66; David Sanger, 87; The Bridgeman Art Library; Rain Forest, Malaysia, 1990 by Laila
Shaws/Private Collection, 12; The Olbatos Ravine, 1967 by Roberto Montenegro, Coleccion Banco National de Mexico,
Photo: Michel Zabe/AZA INBA, 15; Museo Nacional de Antropologia, Mexico City, Mexico/Index, 17; Boltin Picture
Library, 24, 37, 62, 68; Deutsches Tapetenmuseum, Kassei, Germany/Museumlandschaft Hessen Kassel/Gabriele
Boessert, 35; The Creation of Man, page from Popul Vuh(w/c on paper) by Diego Rivera (1886-1957) Museo Casa Diego
Rivera (INBA) Guanajuato, Mexico, Index, © 2008 Banco de Mexico Diego Rivera and Frida Kahlo Museums Trust. Av.
Cinco de Mayo No.2, Col Centro, Del Cuauhtemoc 06059, Mexico D.F.; Scarlet Macaws at a Maya Monument by Nigel
Hughes/Private Collection, 40, 42; Museum of Fine Arts, Houston, Texas/Museum purchase funded by One Great Night
in November 1988, 44; Jungle Parrot by Felicity House/Private Collection, 47; Lovina Ricefields with Lilies and
Frangipanni, Bali, 1996 by Hilary Simon/Private Collection, 48; Further Down The River - The Crocodile, 1982 by Peter
Wilson/Private Collection, 52; Museum of Fine Arts, Houston Texas/Agnes Cullen Arnold Endowment Fund, 54;
Dartmoor (w/c on paper) by Edward Burra (1905-76)/Royal Albert Memorial Museum, Exeter, Devon, UK, 60; Owls illus-
tration from Bird Families by Maruice Burton published by Frederick Warne and Company 1962 by Kay Nixon (1895-
1988), 63; Making Tortillas, 1926 by Diego Rivera (1886-1957) University of California, San Francisco, CA/Index, © 2008
Banco de Mexico Diego Rivera and Frida Kahlo Museums Trust, Av. Cinco de Mayo No.2, Col, Centro, Del.Cuauhtemoc
06059, Mexico, D.F., 65; Museo Nacional de Arqueologia y Ethnologia, Guatemala City/ Jean-Pierre Courau, backcover;
Art Resource: Erich Lessing, 6, 20, 24 (B), 27, 33-34, 56, 57; Schalkwijk, Rivera, Diego (1866-1957) c Banco de Mexico
Trust. The Grinder (La molendera), 1926. Oil on canvas, 35 7/16 x 46 l/16in., 83; Rivera, Diego (1866-1957) © Banco
de Mexico Trust. Corn Festival (la fiesta del maiz), detail 1923-24. Mural court of Fiesta, Level 2 South Wall, 77; Rivera,
Diego (1866-1957) © Banco de Mexico Trust. Water, the Source of Life. The Beneficent Hands of Nature Bestow the
Gift of Water. Carcamo del Rio Lerma, 30; Rivera, Diego (1866-1957) © Banco de Mexico Trust. Sunset (from a series
of twenty painted in Acapulco). 1956. Oil and tempera on canvas 30 x 40 cm, 2-3; Rivera, Diego (1866-1957) © Banco
de Mexico Trust. Corn Harvest, 1923-24. Mural. Court of Fiestas, Level 1, South Wall, 78; SEF, 9, 61, 75. 81, 86; El
Hortelano (1953-) c 2008 Artists Rights Society(ARS), New York/VEGAP, Madrid Big Dipper No 1. 1997. Oil on canvas 75 x 75 cm, 55; Werner Forman, 23, 26, 89.

Printed in Malaysia
135642

Front cover: A Maya warrior
Half-title page: A clay figure of a Maya noble
Title page: A blazing sun sets over the Pacific Ocean, in a painting by the famous Mexican artist
    Diego Rivera.
Back cover: A finely crafted vase from an ancient Maya site in Guatemala

CONTENTS

THE MAGIC *of* MYTHS

EVERY ANCIENT CULTURE HAD ITS MYTHS. These timeless tales of gods and heroes give us a window into the beliefs, values, and practices of people who lived long ago. They can make us think about the BIG QUESTIONS that have confronted humankind down through the ages: questions about human nature, the meaning of life, and what happens after death. On top of all that, myths are simply great stories that are lots of fun to read.

What makes a story a myth? Unlike a narrative written by a particular author, a myth is a traditional story that has been handed down *Above:* from generation to generation, first orally and later in written form. *This clay* Nearly all myths tell the deeds of gods, goddesses, and other divine *container in* beings. These age-old tales were once widely accepted as true and *the shape of* sacred. Their primary purpose was to explain the mysteries of life and *a Maya god* the origins of a society's customs, institutions, and religious rituals. *may have*

been used It is sometimes hard to tell the difference between a myth and a *in sacred* heroic legend. Both myths and legends are traditional stories that may *ceremonies.*

include extraordinary elements such as gods, spirits, magic, and monsters. Both may be partly based on real events in the distant past. However, the main characters in legends are usually mortals rather than divine beings. Another key difference is that legends are basically exciting action stories, while myths almost always express deeper meanings or truths.

Mythology (the whole collection of myths belonging to a society) played an important role in ancient cultures. In very early times, people created myths to explain the awe-inspiring, uncontrollable forces of nature, such as thunder, lightning, darkness, drought, and death. Even after science began to develop more rational explanations for these mysteries, myths continued to provide comforting answers to the many questions that could never be fully resolved. People of nearly all cultures have asked the same basic questions about the world

A war party marches across the walls of a Maya temple dating back to the late eighth century CE

A giant sculpture of a high priest stands in the jungles of Guatemala.

around them. That is why myths from different times and places can be surprisingly similar. For example, the peoples of nearly every ancient culture told stories about the creation of the world, the origins of gods and humans, the cycles of nature, and the afterlife.

Mythology also served ancient cultures as instruction, inspiration, and entertainment. Traditional tales offered a way for the people of a society to express their fundamental beliefs and values and pass them down to future generations. The tales helped preserve memories of a civilization's past glories and held up examples of ideal human qualities and conduct. Finally, these imaginative stories provided enjoyment to countless listeners and readers in ancient times, just as they do today.

The MYTHS OF THE WORLD series explores the mythology of some of history's greatest civilizations. Each book opens with a brief look at the culture that created the myths, including its geographical setting, political history, government, society, and religious beliefs. Next comes the fun part: the stories themselves. We based our retellings of the myths on a variety of traditional sources. The new versions are fun and easy to read. At the same time, we have strived to remain true to the spirit of the ancient tales, preserving their magic, their mystery, and the special ways of speech and avenues of thought that made each culture unique.

As you read the myths, you will come across sidebars, or text boxes, highlighting topics related to each story's characters or themes. The sidebars in *The Ancient Maya* include excerpts from the *Popul Vuh*, a mythological history that is often called the single most important sacred text of the ancient Americas. You will find further information on this ancient text in "About the *Popul Vuh*" on page 89. There is lots of other useful information at the back of the book as well, including a glossary of difficult terms, suggestions for further reading, and more. Finally, the stories are illustrated with both ancient and modern paintings, drawings, sculptures, and other works of art inspired by mythology. These images can help us better understand the spirit of the myths and the way a society's traditional tales have influenced other cultures through the ages.

Now it is time to begin our adventures with the ancient Maya. We hope that you will enjoy this journey to a land where powerful gods and spirits watch over every aspect of life, from the budding of the corn to the movements of the sun, moon, and stars. Most of all, we hope that the sampling of stories and art in this book will inspire you to further explorations of the magical world of mythology.

A dancer wearing an elaborate headdress takes part in a royal celebration.

Part 1

MEET *the*
ANCIENT MAYA

A SACRED LANDSCAPE

THE ANCIENT MAYA (PRONOUNCED MY-uh) LIVED IN A region known today as Mesoamerica. Mesoamerica stretched from the middle of Mexico all the way south to Costa Rica. The Maya lived in the southern part of this large region, in the area that included southern Mexico and all or part of present-day Guatemala, Belize, Honduras, and El Salvador.

The Maya's homeland was a place of great beauty and richly contrasting environments. There were level plains, rolling hills, and rugged mountains. Some areas were covered in lush rain forests, which teemed with jaguars, pumas, monkeys, deer, snakes, and tropical birds. Other areas were nearly as dry as a desert. Snow might cling to a mountain peak in the central highlands while temperatures along the Pacific coast soared to 95 degrees Fahrenheit.

This varied landscape played an important role in the Maya's religious beliefs and myths. Every part of the world—from rocks to trees

Opposite: Palm trees thrived in the dense rain forests of Mesoamerica.

Previous page: Musicians shake rattles made from hollowed-out gourds at the dedication ceremony of a Maya temple.

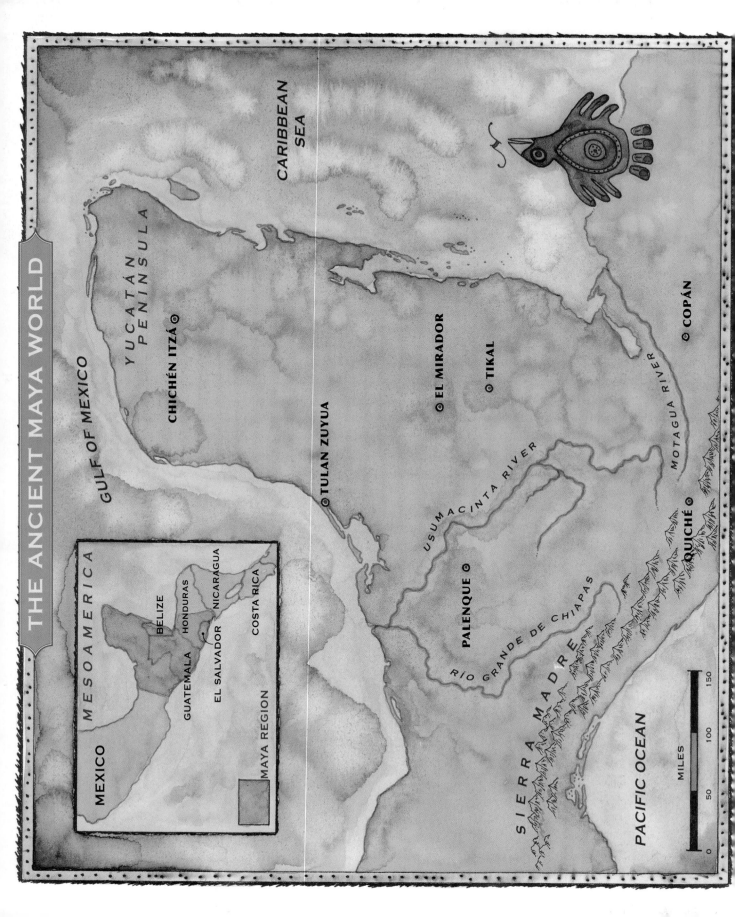

THE ANCIENT MAYA WORLD

CARIBBEAN SEA

GULF OF MEXICO

YUCATÁN PENINSULA

◎ CHICHÉN ITZÁ

◎ EL MIRADOR

◎ TIKAL

◎ COPÁN

◎ TULAN ZUYUA

MOTAGUA RIVER

USUMACINTA RIVER

PALENQUE ◎

RÍO GRANDE DE CHIAPAS

SIERRA MADRE

QUICHÉ ◎

PACIFIC OCEAN

MILES
0   50   100   150

MESOAMERICA

MEXICO

BELIZE

HONDURAS

GUATEMALA

EL SALVADOR

NICARAGUA

COSTA RICA

MAYA REGION

to rivers—was believed to have its own spiritual power. Mountains were especially sacred, because they were regarded as the dwelling places of gods and ancestor spirits. Caves and canyons were entrance-ways to the underworld kingdom known as Xibalba, or "Place of Fright." In "One and Seven Hunahpu" on page 57, two young men disturb the gods of that dreadful realm by playing ball in a canyon.

With all its natural beauty, the ancient Maya world could be unpredictable and dangerous. Volcanoes, earthquakes, and violent coastal storms could strike at any time. Months of nearly constant rainfall alternated with a long dry season, when the land withered and died. This changeable environment helped shaped the Maya's view of the gods and their own place in the world. In "The Great Flood" on page 31, we will learn about an earlier race of humans who were wiped out by floodwaters when they failed to worship the gods.

The ancient Maya might have viewed this ravine as an entrance to the grim underworld or the sacred land of the ancestors.

$\mathcal{A}$ GLORIOUS CIVILIZATION

MESOAMERICA WAS HOME TO A NUMBER OF ANCIENT cultures, including the Olmecs, Zapotecs, Toltecs, Mixtecs, and Aztecs.* The Maya established their first settlements in the region around 2000 BCE. Over the centuries their simple villages developed into one of the most brilliant civilizations of the ancient world.

The Maya civilization was not a single, unified empire. Instead, it was a collection of independent states, each consisting of a city and its surrounding territory. The city-states were fierce rivals that often battled over land, resources, and the control of trade routes. Despite these rivalries, people all over the ancient Maya world shared the same basic way of life, social system, and religious beliefs.

Different parts of the Maya world reached their heights of power and glory at different times. Great city-states such as El Mirador and Tikal emerged in the central region as early as 500 BCE. Other

* To explore the dramatic history and mythology of the Aztecs, see *Myths of the World: The Aztecs.*

A Maya noble
and his servant
celebrate a
military victory.

This pyramid temple in the city of Chichén Itzá was an awe-inspiring setting for sacred rituals.

cities, including Palenque in the west and Copán in the east, thrived during what is known as the Classic period, from around 250 to 900 CE. The people of these and other Maya settlements built magnificent stone palaces and pyramid temples. Skilled artisans created fine paintings, sculptures, pottery, mosaics, and other works of art. Astronomers charted the movements of the planets. Mathematicians developed a complex numerical system. Other great achievements included the invention of remarkably accurate calendars and a sophisticated writing system. Maya writing was based on pictures and symbols called hieroglyphs, which represented words, sounds, and ideas. Through their hieroglyphic writing, the Maya preserved much of their history, beliefs, and myths for future generations.

Between around 800 and 1000 CE, the Maya civilization declined. One city after another was abandoned, for reasons that may have included warfare, overpopulation, famine, and drought. Maya culture did not completely disappear, however. Some people moved to areas in the far north, including the Yucatán Peninsula of Mexico, where powerful cities such as Chichén Itzá flourished. Other Maya moved to the highlands of Guatemala. Among these were the founders of the Quiché kingdom.

In the early 1500s, Spanish soldiers arrived in Mesoamerica on a quest for land and treasure. The invaders brought steel swords, guns, and deadly diseases such as measles and malaria. Within a few decades, an estimated 90 percent of the Maya population had been killed, mostly by disease. Despite the devastation, some isolated cities continued to resist the assault. By the late 1600s, however, the Spanish had conquered the last Maya stronghold.

Even after the Spanish Conquest, the Maya endured. Today millions of their descendants live in Guatemala, Mexico, and neighboring nations. Through these people the traditions, beliefs, and stories of the ancient Maya remain a living part of the modern world.

A Maya ruler wears the elaborate costume of a god associated with war and sacrifice.

A variety of systems of dating have been used by different cultures throughout history. Many historians now prefer to use BCE (Before Common Era) and CE (Common Era) instead of BC (Before Christ) and AD (Anno Domini) out of respect for the diversity of the world's peoples.

KINGS, NOBLES,
and COMMONERS

ANCIENT MAYA SOCIETY WAS DIVIDED INTO TWO CLASSES. Members of the small upper class had most of the wealth and power. Everyone else—about 90 percent of the population—belonged to the lower class.

At the very top of the social order were the kings. The king of a city-state lived at the center of the capital, in an elaborate stone palace. He was the chief political leader, responsible for ensuring the security and prosperity of his subjects through trade, wars, and alliances with other city-states. He also served as the high priest of the state religion. According to ancient Maya beliefs, kings were descended from the gods. Part human and part divine, they had the power to enter the spirit world through religious rituals and ceremonies. Their communications with the supernatural powers protected the people from evil forces and maintained the very order of the universe.

Below the king were the nobles of the upper class, who lived in smaller stone palaces throughout the Maya cities. These privileged people served as the top priests, government officials, and military leaders. Nobles also directed the trade of luxury goods over the paved roads that connected distant Maya regions. Especially gifted nobles might become artist-scribes, honored for their skills in reading and writing.

The lower class was made up of commoners with a variety of occupations. The majority were farmers, laborers, or servants. A smaller group of more prosperous commoners may have included lower-ranking priests, government officials, merchants, soldiers, and skilled craftspeople. Regardless of their occupation, most commoners lived in simple adobe (mud-brick) homes on the outskirts of cities or in farming villages. They had to pay tribute to the king in the form of labor and products.

Maya society was dominated by men. Women were generally expected to marry and devote themselves to their roles as wives and mothers. However, women of all classes enjoyed considerable respect and authority within their homes. Ancient Maya art shows that some upper-class women were educated as scribes. The wives and mothers of kings also played an important part in some religious ceremonies.

A mother carries her young child on her back.

Opposite page: This head of a seventh-century CE king displays the prominent nose and sloping forehead that were the Maya ideal of beauty.

GODS *and* SPIRITS

THE ANCIENT MAYA BELIEVED THAT THE WORLD WAS ALIVE with sacred powers. Everything in the world—rocks, trees, caves, mountains, lakes, rivers—had an invisible sacred quality or spirit. The most powerful spirits took shape in the gods and goddesses who controlled the different parts of the universe.

The Maya gods were complex characters. Every deity was several gods in one, with several different forms and characteristics. He/she could be both male and female, young and old, kindly and cruel. He/she could be represented by a variety of images combining different animal and human features. In addition, people in separate parts of the Maya world often used different names for the same god.

Because of all these contradictions, we are not sure exactly how many gods the Maya worshipped. We do not even know the names of a number of gods shown in ancient Maya art. However, we can describe a few of the most important deities:

The Creator God. No single deity was recognized by all the Maya as the supreme maker of the earth, sky, and humans. The people of the

The image of a bearded sun god decorates an incense burner discovered in the Maya city of Palenque.

Yucatán Peninsula worshipped Itzamna, god of creation, learning, and the arts and sciences. The Quiché Maya of the Guatemalan highlands had two creator gods: Huracan, also called Heart of Sky, and Gucumatz, or the Plumed Serpent.

One of the many gods associated with maize

The Maize God. Maize, or corn, was the chief crop of Mesoamerica and the foundation of the Maya diet. The god of this vital food had several different names and forms. Like most Maya gods, he also had both positive and negative sides. He could be linked with life, prosperity, and fertility, as well as sacrifice and death. The maize god's exceptional powers and qualities made him the special patron of kings.

The Hero Twins. The Hero Twins were brave and clever boy-gods who played a major role in the creation of human beings and the continuing safety and order of the universe. They were associated with the sun, the full moon, and the planet Venus.

The Moon Goddess. The moon was often represented as a goddess with both young and old forms. The Quiché moon goddess was Xquic, or Blood Woman, mother of the Hero Twins.

Chac is one of the oldest and most enduring Maya deities. For thousands of years, he has been adored as the god who brings the rains that nourish the growing crops. Chac can also wield destructive storms and lightning bolts.

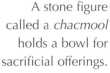

A stone figure called a *chacmool* holds a bowl for sacrificial offerings.

Many other gods were associated with parts of nature and the heavenly bodies. Special deities watched over a variety of human activities. These included the patron gods of warriors, merchants, scribes, hunting, fishing, poetry, and music. Some of the most frightening gods presided over death, war, sacrifice, and the underworld. In this book we will meet the head rulers of the underworld, two grim lords known as One Death and Seven Death.

RITUAL *and* SACRIFICE

RELIGION WAS A VITAL PART OF DAY-TO-DAY LIFE FOR THE ancient Maya. The gods and spirits that inhabited every part of the world could bring rain or drought, health or disease, victory or disaster. Every person, from the lowliest commoner to the king, strived to stay on the good side of these all-powerful beings.

Individuals worshipped the deities through private rituals and offerings. A farmer might recite a prayer to the god of rain before beginning his day's work in the fields. A traveling merchant might burn incense in front of a temporary stone altar, asking the god of commerce to bring him home safely. Families gathered at small household shrines to honor the ancestors who had been reborn as gods to watch over them.

Priests communicated with the gods, spirits, and ancestors on behalf of the entire state. Like the Maya kings, priests were believed

Departed rulers return from the underworld to celebrate the rise of a new king.

to have the power to leave their bodies and journey to the spirit world. Through their otherworldly contacts, they learned the will of the gods, the cause of past events, and the secrets of the future.

Priests also maintained the complex Maya calendars. There were several different calendars, based on different methods of measuring time. A highly accurate 365-day calendar guided the planting and harvesting of crops. A 260-day sacred calendar helped people plan for the future.

Priests interpreted the sacred calendar through a method known as divining. The diviner usually cast lots (seeds or other objects) and

counted them off against the days of the calendar. The foretelling was based on the special meaning of the day that was reached when the lots ran out.

The Maya calendars also determined the dates for a continuous round of religious ceremonies. Public ceremonies were usually conducted outside the temples built at the top of magnificent stone pyramids. Crowds flocked to the plaza below the pyramid during these grand spectacles. They watched as brightly costumed priests and kings worshipped the gods through music, dancing, processions, rituals, and offerings.

Maya religious offerings included gifts of food, drink, and sacrificial birds and animals. The greatest gift of all was human blood. Nobles, priests, and kings offered their blood to the gods by cutting their tongues, lips, cheeks, and other body parts. During very important ceremonies, the Maya performed human sacrifices. Most sacrificial victims were high-ranking nobles captured in war. The Maya believed that their gifts of blood nourished the gods and ensured the continued existence of the world.

Part 2
TIMELESS TALES
of THE MAYA

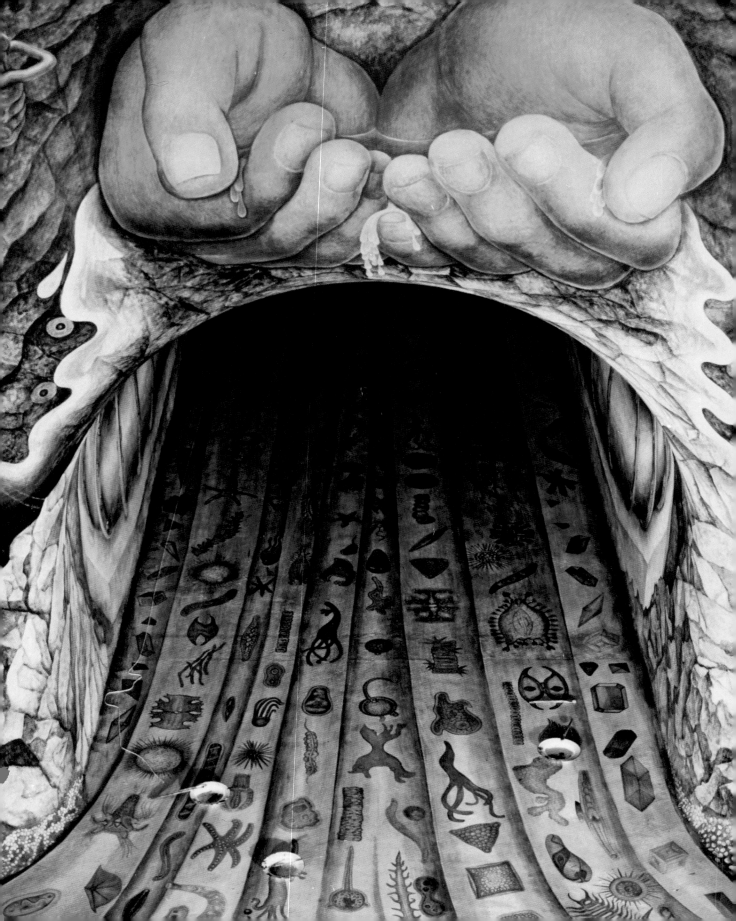

THE ORIGINS
of the WORLD

The Great Flood

NEARLY ALL ANCIENT PEOPLES TOLD STORIES ABOUT the origins of the world and the first humans. The Maya's creation stories have come down to us through words and images painted on clay vessels and inscribed on stone monuments. The Maya also recorded their myths in sacred texts known as codices (KOE-duh-seez). The Maya codices were made of long strips of bark, which were folded like an accordion.

In the early 1500s, the Spanish burned most of the ancient codices in an effort to stamp out the Maya religion. In the midst of this destruction, a few Maya scribes and nobles created new books to preserve their disappearing traditions. These post–Conquest texts included a new edition of an ancient codex called the *Popul Vuh,* or "Council Book."

The *Popul Vuh* was the main sacred text of the Quiché people, who lived in the highlands of Guatemala. The Quiché were one of several Maya groups or nations whose people had their own special heritage and their own dialect, or regional language, descended from an original Maya language. After the Spanish destroyed the *Popul Vuh,*

Opposite:
Divine hands bestow the gift of water, in a painting by Mexican artist Diego Rivera.

Previous page: This Rivera painting is called *Pareja Indigena,* or *Native Couple.*

a small group of Quiché nobles secretly re-created it. The anonymous writers recorded the narrative in the Quiché language, using an alphabetic spelling system adapted from Spanish. Many years later, their manuscript was discovered and translated into other languages. The *Popul Vuh* became our single most important source of ancient Maya mythology.

The myths in this book are based on the *Popul Vuh*'s account of the origins and early history of the world. We begin at the beginning, with the creation of the world and the first creatures. According to this ancient tale, the Maya creator gods had a hard time making a proper population for the earth. Their first three attempts—the animals, a people made from mud, and a people made from wood—were disappointing failures. The gods' struggles give us an insight into the ancient Maya's view of their place in the world. The creatures of earlier ages had to be destroyed because they did not know how to worship their creators. Only by praising the gods and nourishing them with sacrifices could the people of the present world survive and prosper.

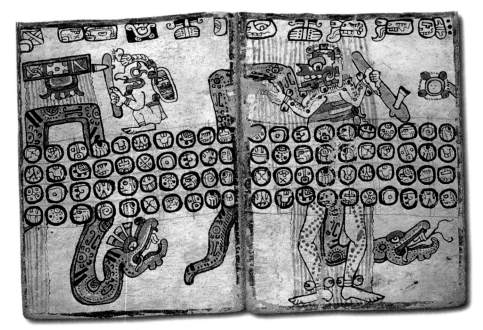

A rain god battles deadly serpents in an illustration from a Maya codex.

CAST *of* CHARACTERS

Gucumatz (goo-koo-MAHTS) God of the sea and creation; also called the **Plumed Serpent**

Huracan (hoo-rah-KAHN) God of the sky and creation; also called **Heart of Sky**

Xpiyacoc (shpee-yah-KAWK) Grandfather of the gods

Xmucane (shmoo-kah-NAY) Grandmother of the gods

HERE IS HOW IT WAS before time began. There was no earth. There was not one rock, tree, or meadow. Not one bird, fish, animal, or person.

There was only the sea, all alone in the darkness. In the sea lay a god, rippling and murmuring. The god was clothed in quetzal feathers, the glittering blue-green feathers that gave him his name: Gucumatz, the Plumed Serpent.

And of course there was the sky above the sea. The blank sky stretched out endlessly over the vast expanse of the waters. In the sky was the god Huracan, whose name means Heart of Sky.

Huracan looked out over the blackness and longed for the dawn. He went down to the sea and spoke to the Plumed Serpent. The gods talked and they thought. In their great wisdom, they dreamed up a vision of how

The Plumed Serpent was adorned with precious quetzal feathers.

the world should be. They saw the earth set apart in the midst of the waters. They saw the growth of trees and bushes. They saw a race of people who would praise them and nurture them with prayers and sacrifices.

Then the gods said, "Earth." And from their word the earth was formed. It arose suddenly, like a cloud billowing up from the waters. Great mountains soared into the sky, dividing the sea into lakes and rivers. The face of the earth sprouted a blanket of cypress and pine trees.

The gods were pleased with their creation. "It is good that you came to me," the Plumed Serpent said to Heart of Sky. "Our design has turned out well. Now let us fill the world with living creatures."

Lush rain forests covered the newly created earth.

So the gods thought of all the animals, small and great. From their thoughts and words, the deer and birds emerged. The gods gave the deer

a home in the meadows, canyons, and forests. They established nests for the birds in the trees and bushes. They also brought forth the jaguars, pumas, serpents, and all the other creatures, giving each a place to live and multiply.

"Now speak out," the gods commanded. "Praise those who have made you." But the animals just squawked and howled and chattered.

The first birds frolicked in the sky, trees, and waters.

"This has not turned out well," said Heart of Sky and the Plumed Serpent. "They cannot name our names and praise us." So the gods told the animals that they would have to serve in another way. They must offer their flesh to be eaten. All the animals, small and great, would become food for the praise givers who had not yet been created.

A second time the gods tried to make a creature who would nurture them with prayers and sacrifices. This time they worked with earth. They mixed the earth with water and formed the mud into the shape of a man. But the creature did not look right. Its face was lopsided, and it could not stand or walk. It could talk, but its words were just sounds without meaning.

"This has not turned out well," said the gods. "Creatures made from mud cannot live and multiply." So Heart of Sky and the Plumed Serpent broke up the image they had created.

Twice the gods had tried and failed to make a praise giver. Before trying a third time, they asked for the help of Grandfather Xpiyacoc and Grandmother Xmucane. These ancient diviners are older than all the other gods. They know how to read the secrets of the universe. "Our grandfather, our grandmother, guide our work," said

Heart of Sky and the Plumed Serpent. "Shall we make a race of people from wood?"

Xpiyacoc and Xmucane set out their lots of coral seeds and corn kernels. They moved their hands over the lots as they counted off the days of the sacred calendar. At last came their answer: "Let there be a race of wooden people."

"So be it," replied the creators. The moment they spoke, it was done. The earth was populated with people made from wood. The bodies of the men were carved from the wood of the coral tree. The women were made from the insides of reeds. At first, the people seemed to be a success. They looked and talked like humans. They multiplied, producing sons and daughters.

But the wooden people had no blood or sweat. Their skin cracked, and their arms and legs warped in the heat. Worst of all, their minds and hearts were empty, so they had no memory of their creators. They just wandered about aimlessly, doing whatever they wanted. They mistreated their animals. They neglected their household utensils, making the millstones screech and burning the cooking pots. They did not call upon their makers in prayer or nurture the gods with sacrifices.

Heart of Sky and the Plumed Serpent were disappointed and angry. The people made from wood were not worthy to live on the face of the earth. So the gods sent a catastrophe to destroy them.

The sky turned black. The rains began to fall. In the midst of the storm came four ferocious demons. Gouger of Faces gouged out the people's eyeballs. Sudden Bloodletter snapped off their heads. Crunching Jaguar ate their flesh. Tearing Jaguar tore apart their bodies.

Those who survived the attack of the

THE BLACK RAINSTORM
BEGAN, RAIN ALL DAY
AND RAIN ALL NIGHT.
~POPUL VUH

The gods sent dreadful demons to punish the faithless wooden people.

demons fled into their houses. Suddenly all their utensils sprang to life. Each and every thing that the people had abused turned against them.

"Pain!" cried the blackened cooking pots. "You set us on fire. Now it is your turn to burn!"

"Pain!" cried the grinding stones. "You wore us down. You rubbed and scraped us against each other. Now we shall grind your flesh!"

"Pain!" cried the dogs. "You kept a stick ready while you ate, so you could hit us when we begged for food. Now it is your turn to be eaten!"

> THEIR HEARTHSTONES WERE SHOOTING OUT, COMING RIGHT OUT OF THE FIRE, GOING FOR THEIR HEADS.
> ⌐POPUL VUH

The desperate wooden people ran out from their homes, into the driving rainstorm. They scrambled up on their roofs, but their houses washed away in the great flood. They climbed the trees, but the branches threw them back to the ground. They tried to hide in the caves, but the stone mouths slammed shut in their faces.

And so the people made from wood were crushed and drowned and scattered. Only a few survived the wrath of the creators. Those few were transformed into monkeys. Today their descendants still scamper through the forests, a reminder of the wooden people who forgot their creators.

THE ANCIENT MAYA SPEAK
The LIGHT *of* HISTORY

The Spanish conquerors of Mesoamerica were determined to wipe out the people's traditional religious beliefs. The Quiché Maya nobles who wrote down the *Popul Vuh* had to work in secrecy in order to protect themselves from punishment. In this introduction to their text, the anonymous writers explain that they must "hide their faces" as they record their people's ancient stories amid the preaching of the new religion, Christianity.

Above: The gods create the first man from mud,
in a Diego Rivera painting inspired by the *Popul Vuh*.

Here we shall write and we shall begin the old stories, the beginning and the origin of all that was done in the town of the Quiché, by the tribes of the Quiché nation.

And here we shall set forth the revelation, the declaration, and the narration of all that was hidden. . . . And [at the same time] the declaration, the combined narration of the Grandmother and the Grandfather, whose names are Xpiyacoc, and Xmucane, helpers and protectors, twice grandmother, twice grandfather, so called in the Quiché chronicles. Then we shall tell all that they did in the light of existence, in the light of history.

This we shall write now under the Law of God and Christianity; we shall bring it to light because now the *Popol Vuh*, as it is called, cannot be seen any more, in which was clearly seen the coming from the other side of the sea and the narration of our obscurity, and our life was clearly seen. There is the original book and ancient writing, but he who reads and ponders it hides his face.

THE HERO TWINS BATTLE EVIL

The Defeat of Seven Macaw

THE *POPUL VUH* CONTINUES ITS TALE OF CREATION IN A gloomy world empty of people. The sun is almost ready to rise for the first time. The creator gods are almost ready to make a proper race of humans. But first two young gods known as the Hero Twins must face a new threat to the divine order of the universe.

The Hero Twins are two of the most revered figures in Maya mythology. In the Quiché language of the *Popul Vuh*, their names are Hunahpu ("First Lord" or "First Hunter") and Xbalanque ("Little Jaguar"). Hunahpu and Xbalanque are culture heroes—mythological characters who help humankind through their acts of courage and discovery. They are also tricksters. Tricksters are entertaining mythological characters who defeat their enemies through a combination of cunning and trickery.

The adventures of the Hero Twins begin with a battle against a conceited bird-god named Vucub Caquix, or "Seven Macaw." A macaw is a brightly colored parrot native to Mesoamerica. Seven Macaw was so bright that he claimed to be the sun and moon. The boy-gods had to

Opposite: Vucub Caquix was the mythical ancestor of these brightly colored scarlet macaws.

destroy this boastful imposter before the real sun could rise and the age of true humans could begin. For help in this important mission, they turned to their grandparents Xpiyacoc and Xmucane, the wise old couple who advised the creator gods in our first story.

The myth of the Hero Twins and Seven Macaw is a warning against the dangers of vanity and arrogance. It also explains a puzzling feature of the night sky. When the bird-god dies, his spirit becomes the seven bright stars of the Big Dipper. In the southern homeland of the ancient Maya, those stars disappear in mid-July, around the start of the rainy season. The Maya associated the setting of the Big Dipper with the downfall of Seven Macaw.

CAST *of* CHARACTERS

Seven Macaw Boastful bird-god; also called **Vucub Caquix** (woo-KOOB kah-KEESH)

Huracan (hoo-rah-KAHN) God of the sky and creation; also called **Heart of Sky**

Hunahpu (hoo-nah-POO)
Xbalanque (shbah-lahn-KAY) } The **Hero Twins**

Chimalmat (tchee-mahl-MAHT) Wife of Seven Macaw

Xpiyacoc (shpee-yah-KAWK) Grandfather of the gods

Xmucane (shmoo-kah-NAY) Grandmother of the gods

AFTER THE WOODEN PEOPLE were destroyed in the great flood, the earth was a sad and gloomy place. The sun had not yet risen. The moon and stars were not yet visible. There was no light of day, no darkness of night, only a long, unchanging twilight.

In this shadowy world, there was one who shined brightly. That was a vain and foolish bird named Vucub Caquix, or "Seven Macaw." Seven Macaw had a shiny white nose and bright silver rings around his eyes. His teeth were encrusted with turquoise and jewels. He lived high in the treetops, in a dazzling metal nest. "My light is brilliant!" he declared, puffing up his lustrous red feathers. "When I stand before my nest, I shine like the sun and moon. I *am* the sun and moon! I will light up the world for humanity."

> "HERE AM I: I AM THE SUN," SAID SEVEN MACAW.
> ⌐POPUL VUH

Seven Macaw's self-glorification offended Huracan. The great creator god wanted to make a new race of humans, but he would not have them worshipping that feathered imposter! So Huracan sent two young gods to rid the world of the boastful bird. He sent Hunahpu and Xbalanque, the Hero Twins.

Hunahpu and Xbalanque were skilled hunters. As they walked on the earth, each boy carried a giant blowgun on his shoulder. "It is no good here without life, without people," they said. "Let's shoot that imposter Seven Macaw. Let's put an end to his jewels, his metals, and all the sources of his brilliance. Then the creators can make the first true mother and father."

So the two young gods observed Seven Macaw. They saw that his favorite food was the fragrant yellow fruit called the nance. The boys took their place beneath a tall nance tree. All night they sat quietly, hidden by the leaves. In the morning, when Seven Macaw came for his breakfast, Hunahpu shot his blowgun.

The stone shot from the blowgun sped through the air. It hit Seven Macaw right in the jaw. With a squawk the bird-god fell flat on the ground. The two boys jumped out from hiding, and Hunahpu ran to finish off their wounded enemy. But Seven Macaw fought back furiously. He grabbed his attacker's arm and yanked it right out of the socket. Then the bird flew home, holding his aching jaw with one claw and clutching the bleeding arm with the other.

"What has happened?" cried Seven Macaw's wife, Chimalmat.

"Hunahpu and Xbalanque shot me!" cried the bird. "They have broken my jaw. Now all my teeth are loose, and the pain is unbearable. At least I got one of their arms. I will hang it up over the fire. I'll be ready when those two tricksters come to get it!"

WHEN SEVEN MACAW ARRIVED, PERCHING OVER HIS MEAL, THE NANCE, IT WAS THEN THAT HE WAS SHOT BY HUNAHPU.
~POPUL VUH

While Seven Macaw plotted his revenge, the Hero Twins were thinking. How could they get back Hunahpu's arm and complete the defeat of their enemy? At last they came up with an idea. They went to visit their grandparents, the wise old diviners Xpiyacoc and Xmucane. "Please help us get our arm back," said the boys. "Go to the home of Seven Macaw and tell him that you are traveling healers. We will follow right behind you, pretending to be harmless children. Meanwhile, you will really be following our instructions."

Xpiyacoc and Xmucane agreed to the plan. They set out for the home of Seven Macaw. As the white-haired couple tottered along, the boys romped and played behind them. Soon they could hear the bird-god yelling his head off in pain and self-pity.

Seven Macaw stopped his moaning when he saw the old couple passing below his nest. "Where are you headed, Grandfather?" he called.

"We're just making our living, your lordship," replied Xpiyacoc.

"But you are old! You should not have to work. Those boys should support you, like proper children."

"Our children are dead, sir. These young boys are our grandchildren. They have no one to care for them, so they follow along behind us. We must travel about, working as healers, to earn a bit of food to feed them."

Seven Macaw's ears perked up. "You are healers? What illnesses can you treat?"

"We just heal eyes and bones and teeth, your lordship."

"Please, cure my teeth!" cried the bird. "Two tricksters shot me, and ever since then, my life has been misery. I cannot eat and I cannot sleep. I implore you, take pity on my suffering!"

Grandfather and Grandmother pretended to examine Seven Macaw's broken jaw. "It is a worm," they said. "A worm is gnawing at the jawbone. We can remove it. It is merely a matter of pulling out all your teeth."

The vain bird was not sure that he wanted his teeth removed. "I am, after all, a great lord," he said nervously. "My beautiful teeth are signs of my wealth and glory."

"Don't worry, we'll replace them with false teeth made from the very finest ground bone. Your teeth will look as good as new. Or would you rather suffer forever?"

"Oh, very well. I can't bear the pain any longer! Yank them out!" said Seven Macaw.

So Grandfather and Grandmother cured Seven Macaw's toothache. They pulled out every one of the beautiful teeth that glittered with turquoise and jewels. As replacements they put in kernels of soft white corn. The bird's cheeks caved in, and his mouth lost all its splendor.

Next the healers cured Seven Macaw's eyes. They trimmed away the silver rings that had made the bird's eyes shine so brightly. As they worked, their foolish patient felt no pain, no suspicion. He simply sat there as the last of his finery was taken from him, just as the clever twins Hunahpu and Xbalanque had intended.

Now Seven Macaw no longer looked or felt like a lord. Without the gems and metals that had given him his glory, he was nothing. He quickly wasted away and died. His spirit rose into the northern sky, where it became the seven stars of the Big Dipper. When Chimalmat died, she joined her husband in the sky as the Little Dipper.

The spirit of the shining bird-god was transformed into seven bright stars.

THE LAST OF HIS TEETH CAME OUT, THE
JEWELS THAT HAD STOOD OUT BLUE FROM
HIS MOUTH. . . .
SUCH WAS THE
LOSS OF THE
RICHES OF
SEVEN MACAW.
⁓*POPUL VUH*

Today the descendants of Seven Macaw still live on the earth. They are the noisy red birds known as scarlet macaws. The white circles around their eyes and their odd toothless jaws remind us of the fall of their arrogant ancestor.

And what about the Hero Twins? When Seven Macaw died, Grandmother and Grandfather retrieved Hunahpu's arm from its spot above the fire. They put the arm back in place, and the break healed perfectly.

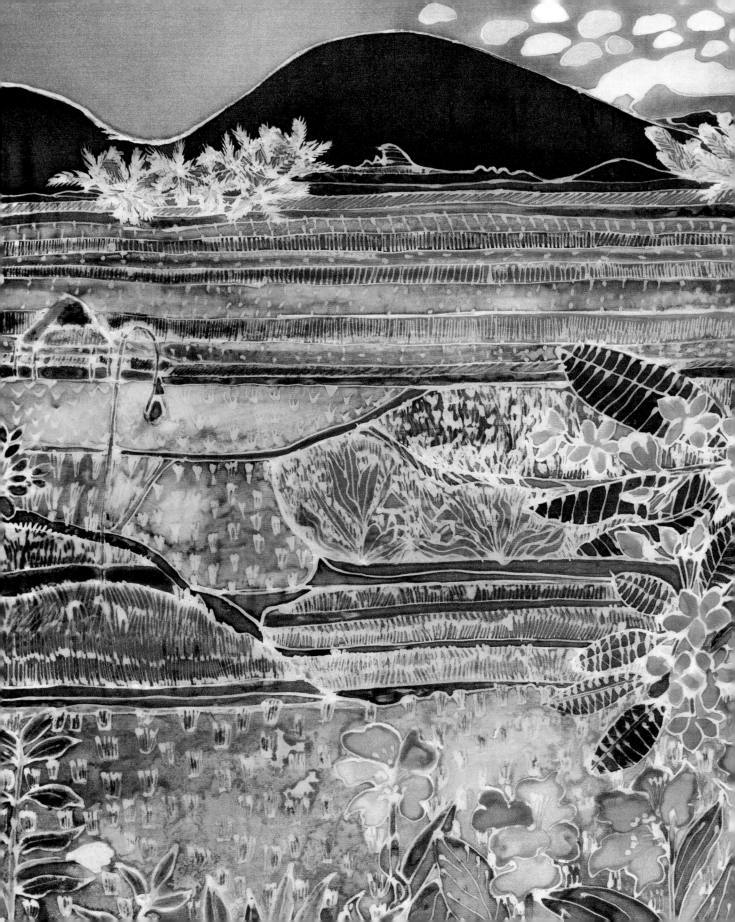

The HERO TWINS OUTSMART the GIANTS

Zipacna and Earthquake

THE DEFEAT OF SEVEN MACAW WAS NOT THE END OF the Hero Twins' fight against evil. The heroic tricksters still had to deal with the bird-god's sons, Zipacna and Cabracan. Zipacna was a crocodile-like giant who had the power to make mountains. He falsely claimed to have created the earth itself, as well as the mountains. Cabracan, whose name means "Earthquake," delighted in knocking down his brother's mountains. He inflated his powers by boasting that he could destroy the sky and earth. The arrogance of these two pretenders offended the creator gods and upset the proper order of the universe.

To rid the world of the giants, the creators turned to Hunahpu and Xbalanque, the Hero Twins. First the boy-gods lured Zipacna into a cave, where he was trapped and turned to stone. Then they tricked Earthquake by casting a magic spell on his dinner. They shot a bird and baked it in a coating of earth. When the giant ate the enchanted meal, he was doomed to end up covered by earth himself.

Opposite: The rolling hills and mountains were created by the boastful giant Zipacna.

The Hero Twins' victory over Zipacna and Earthquake once again reminds us of the perils of false pride. Like their father, the two giants sealed their fate when they dared to proclaim themselves equal to the gods. While Seven Macaw rose into the sky after his death, his sons were buried safely beneath the earth. From time to time, though, Cabracan could still cause trouble. It was his movements in the grave that brought the earthquakes that shook the Maya world.

CAST *of* CHARACTERS

Hunahpu (hoo-nah-POO)
Xbalanque (shbah-lahn-KAY) } The **Hero Twins**

Seven Macaw Boastful bird-god; also called **Vucub Caquix** (woo-KOOB kah-KEESH)

Zipacna (see-pahk-NAH) Elder son of Seven Macaw

Cabracan (kah-brah-KAHN) Younger son of Seven Macaw; also called **Earthquake**

Huracan (hoo-rah-KAHN) God of the sky and creation; also called **Heart of Sky**

HUNAHPU AND XBALANQUE had defeated Seven Macaw, the bird whose self-glorification had offended the creators. But their task was not yet finished. Seven Macaw had left behind two sons, and they were just as arrogant and dangerous as their father.

The elder son was called Zipacna. Zipacna was a powerful giant who went around piling up the surface of the earth into mountains. "Here am I. I am the maker of mountains. I am the maker of the earth!" he boasted.

The second son was called Cabracan, or "Earthquake." He roamed the world destroying everything his brother created. With a tap of his foot, this mighty giant could make the earth shake and the mountains tumble down. "Here am I. I am the breaker of mountains. I can bring down the sky and destroy the earth with avalanches!" bragged Earthquake.

> JUST BY LIGHTLY TAPPING HIS FOOT ON THE GROUND [EARTHQUAKE] INSTANTLY DEMOLISHES THE MOUNTAINS.
> ⁓*POPUL VUH*

The Hero Twins saw the evil in the false claims of the two giants. They knew that the true creators could not make a new race of humans until the arrogant pretenders were defeated. So they came up with a plan to overthrow the elder son, Zipacna.

Every day Zipacna hunted for fish and crabs along the shores of a river. Hunahpu and Xbalanque decided to lure the giant to his death with a counterfeit crab. They used a large flat stone to make the crab's shell. They used red stems and flowers for the arms and claws. They placed the fake crab in a cave at the base of a tall mountain in the west.

After that the crafty boys went walking along the shore. They found Zipacna lying in the water with only his eyes and nose protruding,

Zipacna looked like a crocodile as he lurked in the shallow water.

just like a crocodile. "What are you doing?" the Hero Twins asked.

"I'm hunting for my food, boys," replied the giant.

"What do you eat?"

"Fish and crabs. But it has been two days since I found any. I can hardly stand the hunger."

"Well, there *is* that crab down in the cave. It's a really big one! We wanted to catch it, but we were afraid we'd get bitten."

"Don't be so timid, boys," said the giant. "Come along and point out this splendid crab to me."

So Hunahpu and Xbalanque led Zipacna back along the river. They came to the foot of the great western mountain. The giant looked into the cave and saw the gleaming shell of the crab. "Very good," he said. "That will cure my hunger!"

Zipacna entered the cave. He wriggled in on his back until only his kneecaps were showing, but he still couldn't reach the big, tempting crab. He took a deep breath and squeezed in a bit farther. When he let out his breath, he was wedged in tight. He couldn't turn over. He couldn't get back out. The weight of the great mountain lay on his chest until Zipacna himself turned to stone.

Now only one member of Seven Macaw's family of boasters was left. Only the second son, the one called Earthquake, remained to be defeated. Huracan himself complained to the Hero Twins about Earthquake. "That giant is growing even larger and heavier than the sun I am making," said the god.

"That should not be. It isn't right for a giant to place himself above the great creator," said the two boys. So off they went to rid the world of the troublemaker.

Hunahpu and Xbalanque met up with Earthquake at the foot of a mountain. He was stamping his foot on the ground. "What are you doing?" they asked him.

"I am demolishing mountains, boys," replied the giant. "I am the one who breaks them up, day after day, so that not one is left standing." Earthquake peered into their faces. "I haven't seen you before. What are your names? Where do you come from?"

"We have no names. We're just poor, nameless orphans. We make our way through the forests, hunting and trapping. In our travels we have seen a new mountain growing in the east. It is swelling up, taller than all the others. How can that be, since you claim to be such a mighty destroyer of mountains?"

"Where is this splendid mountain?" rumbled Earthquake. "Lead me to it. You'll see me knock it down yet."

So the Hero Twins led the giant far to the east. As the boy-gods walked along, they practiced their shooting. Earthquake was amazed by their skill as hunters. They simply blew through their blowguns, and the birds toppled from the treetops.

After a while the twins stopped to make dinner. They prepared the birds they had shot, covering one with a most unusual topping: plaster made from ground-up rocks and earth. As they worked on this bird, they cast a powerful spell on it. "This is the one we must give to the giant when he gets hungry," they whispered. "In earth we will cook it. In earth will be his grave. When he eats this bird, we will have our victory."

Then Hunahpu and Xbalanque set the meal over the fire. The plump, juicy flesh roasted over the crackling flames. Soon the birds were brown and tender, and the air was filled with an irresistible aroma.

Earthquake sniffed. His giant mouth watered. When he spoke, he sprayed the boys with his spittle. "What are you cooking there? I smell something truly delicious! Please give me a little taste of it!"

So they gave the earth-covered bird to Earthquake. The moment he took his first bite, he was as good as defeated. The greedy giant ate the whole thing, flesh and bones and coating. When he was finished, he licked his greasy fingers. Then the three travelers continued on their journey. They walked all the way to the foot of the great eastern mountain.

The giant gazed up at the mountain. Too late he realized that he had lost all the strength in his arms and legs. He could not destroy the mountain. He could not even resist when the Hero Twins bound him. The boy-gods tied the giant's hands behind his back. They tied his ankles to his wrists. Then they dug a deep hole and buried him alive, with a heap of earth as his covering.

So it was that the Hero Twins defeated the sons of Seven Macaw, who had claimed to be as great as the creators. To this day Zipacna rests beneath the mountain in the west, and his younger brother lies buried in the east. From time to time, Earthquake shifts restlessly in his grave. That is when the surface of the earth shakes and the mountains tremble.

The Hero Twins covered the bird with earth and baked it over the fire.

The FOUR HUNDRED BOYS

The *Popul Vuh* illustrates Zipacna's destructive power with a story about a group of gods known as the Four Hundred Boys. The Four Hundred Boys were the gods of alcohol and drunkenness. Alarmed by Zipacna's great strength, they decided to kill him before he could harm them. In the following passage, the giant is digging a hole when they drop a log on him. He survives the attack by hiding in a side tunnel. Later he climbs out and drops their house on them. Following their deaths, the boy-gods become the Pleiades, a group of bright stars that the Quiché Maya call Motz ("four hundred").

When [the Four Hundred Boys] had dug a hole, one that went deep, they called for Zipacna:

"We're asking you to please go on digging out the dirt. We can't go on," he was told.

"Very well," he replied.

After that he went down in the hole.

"Call out when enough dirt has been dug, when you're getting down deep," he was told.

"Yes," he replied, then he began digging the hole. But the only hole he dug was for his own salvation. He realized that he was to be killed, so he dug a separate hole to one side, he dug a second hole for safety. . . .

Meanwhile, a big log is being dragged along by the boys.

And then they threw the log down in the hole. . . .

Now [Zipacna] gave a single cry. He called out when the log fell to the bottom.

"Right on! He's been finished!"

"Very good! We've done him in, he's dead. . . . On to the making of our sweet drink! . . ."

All the boys got drunk, and once they were drunk, all four hundred of those boys, they weren't feeling a thing.

After that the [house] was brought down on top of them by Zipacna. All of them were completely flattened. . . .

Such was the death of those Four Hundred Boys. And it used to be said that they entered a constellation, named Motz after them.

Above: The Four Hundred Boys became the glittering cluster of stars known as the Pleiades.

ADVENTURES *in* *the* UNDERWORLD

One and Seven Hunahpu

THE *POPUL VUH* FOLLOWS ITS ACCOUNT OF THE HERO
Twins' exploits on earth with a myth that takes place mainly in the
underworld. This story is so long that we have divided it into two chap-
ters. In this chapter we step back in time to the events that led up to
the twins' birth. In the next chapter, we will learn about the boy-gods'
greatest adventure, their battle against the lords of death.

Our story begins with an earlier set of twins, One Hunahpu and
Seven Hunahpu. These two young gods were expert ballplayers. The
noise of their playing disturbed the lords of the underworld realm of
Xibalba (she-bahl-BAH), or "Place of Fright." The lords summoned
One and Seven Hunahpu to Xibalba and put them through a series of
seemingly impossible challenges. After failing the tests, the brothers
were sacrificed at the underworld ball court. One Hunahpu's severed
head was placed in a dead tree, which miraculously began to bear fruit.
When an underworld maiden named Blood Woman tried to pick the
fruit, she became pregnant. Blood Woman escaped to the upper

Opposite:
The Maya ball
game was part
entertainment,
part religious
spectacle.
In this stone
carving, a
ballplayer
throws a
rubber ball
shaped like
a turtle.

world, where she gave birth to One Hunahpu's sons, the boy-gods who would become known as the Hero Twins.

The adventures of One and Seven Hunahpu give us a window into some of the ancient Maya's ideas about death and sacrifice. Despite its grim name, Xibalba was usually seen more as a place of rest than fright. Just as the two brothers had to overcome a series of obstacles during their descent to Xibalba, the souls of people who died faced many difficult trials on their journey to a peaceful afterlife.

After death One Hunahpu's head still had enough sacred power to father the Hero Twins. This reflects the ancient Maya's belief in the life-giving power of blood and sacrifice. According to this view, the death of a sacrificial victim was not an ending but a transformation that created new life out of old.

CAST *of* CHARACTERS

One Hunahpu (hoo-nah-POO) Father of the Hero Twins
Seven Hunahpu Twin brother of One Hunahpu
Xpiyacoc (shpee-yah-KAWK) Grandfather of the gods
Xmucane (shmoo-kah-NAY) Grandmother of the gods
One Death
Seven Death } Head lords of Xibalba
Blood Woman Mother of the Hero Twins; also called **Xquic**
Blood Gatherer One of the demon lords of Xibalba
Hunahpu
Xbalanque (shbah-lahn-KAY) } The **Hero Twins**

The Descent to Xibalba

ONE HUNAHPU AND HIS BROTHER, SEVEN HUNAHPU, were the twin sons of the wise old couple Xpiyacoc and Xmucane. More than anything else, the two brothers liked to play ball. They played every day, until they became the finest ballplayers in all the world.

The ball court where One Hunahpu and Seven Hunahpu played was at the eastern edge of the earth, in a place called Great Abyss. Below Great Abyss was the grim underworld realm of Xibalba. The noise from the brothers' games annoyed the chief lords of Xibalba, One Death and Seven Death.

"What's all that racket?" the lords complained. "Who disturbs our peace with their stomping and shouting? Let them come here to play ball. We'll teach them to show us some respect!"

So One and Seven Death sent four monstrous owls to summon One and Seven Hunahpu to Xibalba. The winged messengers flew up to the ball court where the young men were playing. They repeated their masters' words: "Come play ball with us here. Bring along all your gaming equipment."

The young men did not dare disobey such a summons. Still, they did not trust the lords of the dead. So they went to their house and hid their valuable ball-playing gear in the rafters. "Don't be sad, dear mother," they told Xmucane. "We're going down to the underworld, but we will return."

Then One and Seven Hunahpu followed the messenger owls down to Xibalba. The way was long and filled with obstacles. They had to descend a steep cliff and pass through rapids churning with sharp spikes. They had to cross a river of blood and a river of flowing pus. They made it safely to a crossroads where four roads met. It was there that their doom was

One and Seven Hunahpu followed the treacherous path down to Xibalba.

sealed. When the Black Road whispered "Follow me," the brothers listened. They took the Black Road, and that was the path of no return.

At last One and Seven Hunahpu came to the council place of Xibalba. They saw all the hideous demon lords seated on thrones, still as statues. The young men greeted the first two demons politely. The figures did not move. They did not answer. They were just wooden manikins!

Suddenly the rest of the figures burst out laughing. How easily they had fooled their two visitors! "Please forgive our small joke," said One and Seven Death. "You must be tired after your long journey. Sit here on our bench and rest."

The two brothers sat down on the bench. It was burning hot! They jumped up, holding their scorched bottoms. At that, the lords of Xibalba fell down laughing. They rolled around on the ground,

> THE LORDS OF XIBALBA . . . SHOUTED WITH LAUGHTER BECAUSE THEY HAD TRIUMPHED [OVER] ONE AND SEVEN HUNAHPU.
> ⌐POPUL VUH

shrieking and howling until their skulls rattled.

Now it was time for a more deadly test. One and Seven Hunahpu must spend the night in a house of utter darkness. As they entered Dark House, they were given a torch and two cigars. "Keep these burning all night," the demon lords told them. "In the morning you must return them just as they look now."

The demon lords forced the brothers to endure a series of challenges.

All that night One and Seven Hunahpu crouched in Dark House. They watched their torch and cigars burn down to ashes. In the morning they were taken before One and Seven Death.

"Where is our torch? Where are our cigars?" the demons asked.

"We finished them, your lordships."

"Then you are finished, too. This very day you will die."

So the brothers were taken to the ball court of Xibalba. There they were sacrificed and buried. Before burying the bodies, the lords cut off the head of One Hunahpu. They placed the head in the fork of a dead tree, as a token of their victory.

All of a sudden, the tree began to bear fruit. Soon it was covered with large, round, hard-shelled calabash. When One and Seven Death saw the miraculous tree, they were worried. They passed a decree: "Let no one go beneath the calabash tree. Let no one pick its fruit."

One maiden would defy that decree. Her name was Blood Woman, and her act of disobedience would mean doom for the lords of Xibalba.

The Birth of the Hero Twins

BLOOD WOMAN WAS THE DAUGHTER of an underworld demon named Blood Gatherer. The maiden was as beautiful as her father was repulsive. She also had a rebellious nature. When she heard about the forbidden calabash tree, she just had to see it for herself.

The maiden went all alone to the ball court of Xibalba. There she saw the amazing calabash tree. "These fruit should be picked," she said. "Their sweetness is going to waste."

Suddenly a voice came from the tree: "If you want the fruit, stretch out your right hand."

Blood Woman reached out her hand to the speaking calabash. The fruit spit in her palm. When she pulled back her hand, she found that the palm was dry. Then she heard the voice again, and when she looked, the fruit had turned into a gruesome skull.

"Do not be afraid," said the skull. "My spittle is a sign that I have given you. When a man dies, the flesh leaves his skull, but he does not disappear. His substance lives on in his sons and daughters. So it is that I will live through you."

Blood Woman returned home. She kept everything that she had seen and heard secret in her heart. Six months passed, and her belly grew big with the child that had been placed in her through the spittle of One Hunahpu.

The severed head of One Hunahpu spit into Blood Woman's hand.

When Blood Gatherer saw that his daughter was with child, he was furious. He became even angrier when she would not tell him the name of the father. "My daughter has brought shame on herself and her entire family," the demon told the four great owls of Xibalba. "Take

THE OWLS . . . TOOK THE MAIDEN BY THE HAND, BRINGING ALONG THE WHITE DAGGER, THE INSTRUMENT OF SACRIFICE.

⁓*POPUL VUH*

her away and sacrifice her. Bring back her heart in this bowl, so that all the lords will know she is dead."

So the owls led Blood Woman away. But before they could sacrifice her, the maiden spoke to them: "Do not kill me, messengers! What I bear in my belly is no disgrace, but the child of One Hunahpu. It was begotten when I went to marvel at the calabash tree."

"We do not want to kill you," said the owls, "but we were told to bring your heart to the lords of Xibalba."

"My heart does not belong to them," said the maiden. Then she gathered up the thick red sap of the croton tree. She shaped the sap into a round ball that looked just like a heart. When she rolled the ball around in the bowl, it formed a bright red coating that glistened like blood.

The owls took the bowl to the council place. The lords of Xibalba placed the fake heart over the sacrificial fire. They leaned over the fire and breathed in the fragrance. The smoke of the blood was truly sweet!

While the lords savored their sacrifice, the owls helped Blood Woman escape from Xibalba. They sent her up through a hole, onto the surface of the earth. The maiden went to the house of Xmucane, mother of One and Seven Hunahpu.

The owls did not want to kill Blood Woman.

"Your sons are not dead. Their light lives on in the children I carry," the maiden told the old woman.

"Very well, if you are my daughter-in-law, prove it! Make yourself useful. Go to the garden and fill this carrying net with corn."

Blood Woman took the net and went to the garden. There was only one maize plant, bearing one ear of corn. "Unfortunate me!" she exclaimed. "Where will I get the food that my mother-in-law asked for?"

In her despair the maiden called on the goddesses who watch over the growing crops:

Come thou, rise up, come thou, stand up.
Generous Woman, Harvest Woman,
Cacao Woman, Cornmeal Woman,
Thou guardians of the food!

Then Blood Woman took hold of the silken tassels at the top of the corn. The ear came away in her hand, and another one took its place. Again and again she pulled on the silk. Again and again another ear appeared. Soon the big net was filled with corn.

When the maiden returned with the load of corn, Xmucane was amazed. The old woman went to look at the garden. She saw the one stalk of corn still standing. At the foot of the stalk was the imprint that the net had left in the soil.

Grandmother Xmucane was a skilled diviner. She knew that the mark of the net was a sign that One Hunahpu would rise again. "You really are my daughter-in-law!" she said to the maiden. "I will soon see my grandchildren, and they will fulfill a great destiny."

So Blood Woman stayed with Xmucane until the day came for the birth of the children. They were born in the mountains, on the day called Net. Two boys were born, and they were named Hunahpu and Xbalanque, the Hero Twins.

The ears of corn
gathered by Blood
Woman would
be used to make
tortillas and other
good foods.

The HERO TWINS DEFEAT DEATH

Playing Ball with the Lords of Xibalba

ONE AND SEVEN HUNAHPU HAD FAILED IN THEIR struggle against the gods of Xibalba. Through their defeat, however, they had paved the way for the triumph of the Hero Twins. After some childhood adventures, these remarkable boys discovered the ball-playing equipment hidden by their father and uncle. With that discovery they realized their destiny: to challenge the lords of death.

Like One and Seven Hunahpu, the Hero Twins traveled down to the underworld. Through a combination of cleverness and magic, they passed the tests that their father and uncle had failed. They also survived a number of other trials, including a ball game against the lords of death. Then the boy-gods tricked their opponents into submitting to sacrifice. With this clever feat, the Hero Twins conquered death itself. Following their victory, they rose into the sky, where they became the sun and the full moon (or, in some versions of the story, the sun and the planet Venus).

Opposite:
The kneeling man in this temple painting is a prisoner of war. Like the Hero Twins, war captives were often sacrificed at the ball court.

It is no accident that some of the Hero Twins' most exciting adventures took place on the ball court. Every major Maya city had a large stone court where the ball game was played. The exact rules of this ancient game are unknown. The object may have been to knock a solid rubber ball through stone rings mounted on the walls. The players could hit the ball with any part of the body except their hands and feet.

The Maya ball game was much more than an entertaining sport. It was also a sacred religious ritual. Ball courts were believed to be points of entry to the underworld. Ball games re-created the battle between the Hero Twins and the lords of death. Sometimes the players on one side were prisoners of war who had been weakened through starvation or injury in order to ensure their defeat. After the game the losing players were beheaded. These sacrifices honored the gods of life and fertility and celebrated the Hero Twins' victory over death.

A clay ballplayer in action, from around 600 CE

CAST *of* CHARACTERS

Hunahpu (hoo-nah-POO)
Xbalanque (shbah-lahn-KAY) } The **Hero Twins**

One Monkey
One Artisan } Firstborn sons of One Hunahpu; patron gods of arts and crafts

One Hunahpu Father of the Hero Twins

Seven Hunahpu Twin brother of One Hunahpu

One Death
Seven Death } Head lords of Xibalba

Huracan (hoo-rah-KAHN) God of the sky and creation; also called **Heart of Sky**

A Great Destiny

HUNAHPU AND XBALANQUE, THE HERO TWINS, grew up strong, wise, and clever. When they were still children, they proved their special qualities by vanquishing their half brothers, One Monkey and One Artisan. The older boys were the firstborn sons of One Hunahpu. They were jealous of their younger brothers and treated them cruelly. The twins got even by tricking their brothers into climbing a tall tree, then turning them into monkeys.

When they got older, Hunahpu and Xbalanque decided to plant a garden. They took up their ax and hoe and went out into the forest. They stuck the ax in the trunk of a tree, and it cut down the tree by itself. They stuck the hoe in the ground, and it began to dig up the weeds and brambles. In just one day, the ax and hoe cleared the ground and made it ready for planting.

The next morning Hunahpu and Xbalanque returned to the clearing. Every tree, bush, and weed had grown up high again! The twins had to start all over. Just as before, their tools cleared the forest and prepared the ground for the garden.

That night the brothers hid behind some trees and kept watch. In the middle of the night, they saw animals creep into the clearing. Small and great, the creatures gathered: pumas, jaguars, deer, rabbits, foxes, coyotes, little birds, large birds. They began to chant: "Arise, you trees! Arise, you bushes!" Their magical chant made all the plants grow again.

All but the rat escaped into the forest.

Quickly the boys jumped out from hiding. They grabbed the deer and the rabbit by the tail, but the tails broke off in their hands. (That is why deer and rabbits have shortened tails.) The rest of the animals escaped into the forest—all but the rat. Hunahpu and Xbalanque caught him in their net. In their anger they held him over the fire. All the hair on his tail was burned off (and to this day, the rat has a hairless tail).

"Let me go!" cried the rat. "Give me some food, and I will tell you a secret."

"Go ahead and tell us," said the boys.

"Very well. Your father and uncle were great ballplayers who died in Xibalba. It is your destiny to go down to the underworld and avenge them. You will find their gaming equipment hidden up in the rafters of the house."

Hunahpu and Xbalanque were overjoyed when they heard the rat's story. They set him free, promising that from that day on, he would always have his share of the stored crops. Then they went to their grandmother's house and found the gaming equipment. They took the gear to the ball court at Great Abyss, where One and Seven Hunahpu had once played. After that the Hero Twins practiced every day, until they were even greater players than their father and uncle before them.

A Deadly Ball Game

WHO IS PLAYING BALL UP THERE NOW?" asked the lords of Xibalba. "Don't they know that One and Seven Hunahpu died for disturbing us?"

Then, just as before, One and Seven Death sent their monstrous owls to earth. The four messengers flew up to the house where the Hero Twins lived with their mother and grandmother. "You are summoned to the underworld," the owls told the boys. "Bring all your gaming equipment. In seven days' time, you will play ball with the masters of Xibalba."

The Hero Twins were happy to obey the lords' summons. First they said good-bye to their mother and grandmother. Then they followed the same path as their father and uncle. They descended the cliff, passed through the rapids, and crossed over Blood River and Pus River. They came to the crossroads. But they did not listen to the Black Road, because they knew that it had lured One and Seven Hunahpu to their deaths. Instead, the boy-gods took another road to Xibalba.

The demon lords sat waiting in the council place. Before entering, the clever boys sent a mosquito ahead to spy for them. The little insect bit the lords, one by one. The first two figures did not make a sound. The others cried out, calling to one another by name. The mosquito flew back and told the boys what had happened. Thus the Hero Twins were not deceived when they came before the council. They ignored the two wooden manikins and addressed each of the real lords by name.

Next came the trick of the hot bench. The boys weren't fooled by that, either. When One Death and Seven Death told them to sit, they said, "No thanks! That's just a hot stone for cooking!"

After that the twins entered Dark House. Like their father and uncle, they were given a torch and two cigars. The clever boys substituted the bright red tail feathers of a macaw for the flame of the torch. As for the cigars, they put fireflies on the tips. In the morning the torch and cigars looked just like new.

Now the lords of death whispered among themselves: "Who are these strangers? How do they keep winning out over us? Let's play ball. We will defeat them on the ball court of Xibalba!"

So the Hero Twins and the lords of death took their places on the ball court. The demons insisted on using a human skull as the ball. When Hunahpu hit the skull-ball, the bones shattered. A sharp stone

THE WHITE DAGGER . . . WENT CLATTERING, TWISTING ALL OVER THE FLOOR OF THE COURT.

~POPUL VUH

dagger came flying out. The dagger clattered all over the floor of the court, but the boys managed to escape its deadly point.

Next the twins' rubber ball was put into play. Although Hunahpu and Xbalanque were better players than the lords, they let themselves lose. They were ready to move on to their real mission: not to win a ball game but to avenge the deaths of One and Seven Hunahpu.

"We've done well! We've beaten them!" exclaimed the lords of Xibalba. "Now we will play an even more deadly game."

Then the lords forced Hunahpu and Xbalanque to endure a new series of challenges. First the twins had to spend the night in Razor House, where sharp blades tried to cut them to pieces. The blades stopped moving when the boys promised to give them the flesh of animals to eat instead. The next night the Hero Twins entered Cold House. Their bodies were so filled with warmth and energy that they did not even feel the freezing winds and hail. The boys also survived the tests of Jaguar House and the House of Fire.

The final ordeal was Bat House. Monstrous bats with snouts like knives filled this dreadful place. The boy-gods used their magic to make themselves small. They spent the night hiding inside their blowguns. Just before morning Hunahpu crawled to the mouth of his gun

The demons played ball with a human skull that concealed a lethal dagger.

One of the sharp-toothed bats inside Bat House snatched off Hunahpu's head.

and peeked out. *Whoosh!* A bat swooped down and bit off his head!

The demons rejoiced as they rolled the head of Hunahpu onto the ball court. Meanwhile, Xbalanque was busy. He found a squash and carved it into the shape of a head. He called on Huracan, and the great god came down from the sky and filled the hollow squash with brains. Then Xbalanque placed the carving on his brother's shoulders.

Day was just about to dawn when the Hero Twins arrived at the ball court. The demons were surprised to see Hunahpu walking about again, but they were sure they could beat a player with a squash for a head. "We've won! You're done!" They laughed as they dropped their ball into play. The ball was the head of Hunahpu!

Xbalanque hit the ball hard, and it took off into the trees. Quickly the two boys ran to recover it. They switched the real head and the carved squash. Xbalanque placed the head on Hunahpu's shoulders and tossed the squash into play on the court. After a few hits, the squash-ball split open, spilling its seeds. With that, the masters of Xibalba knew that the Hero Twins had outsmarted them again.

Now the lords were very angry. With all their tricks, they had not been able to defeat the Hero Twins. So they came up with one last plan. They dug a pit and filled it with branches. They lit the wood on fire. "Let's try a new contest," they told the boys. "Let's take turns jumping over the bonfire."

Hunahpu and Xbalanque were ready to die, but not in the way the lords of Xibalba intended. "You can't fool us," they said cheerfully. "Watch!" Then they jumped into the fiery pit and died together.

All the demon lords whistled and shouted: "At last we have overcome them!" When the fire died down, they took the boys' bones and crushed them on a grinding stone. They sprinkled the ground bones in the river. Then they held a fiesta to celebrate their triumph over the Hero Twins.

The Hero Twins Conquer Death

THE HERO TWINS were not really defeated. Their bones just sank to the bottom of the river and turned back into boys. Five days later, Hunahpu and Xbalanque reappeared. Disguised as wandering performers, they presented themselves at the court of Xibalba. They sang and danced and performed magic tricks. Their best trick

The Hero Twins tricked the lords of Xibalba into offering themselves for sacrifice.

was the human sacrifice. Hunahpu lay down on the sacrificial stone. Xbalanque cut open his brother's chest and took out the heart. "Get up!" he said, and instantly Hunahpu came back to life.

The lords of Xibalba applauded wildly when they saw the amazing trick. They longed to try it themselves. "Do it to us! Sacrifice us!" One and Seven Death shouted.

"Very well, your lordships. After all, what do you have to fear from death?" And the Hero Twins sacrificed One and Seven Death. But this time the sacrifice was for real. The two lords did not come back to life.

Now the boys removed their disguises and revealed themselves to the remaining demons. "Hear our names. We are Hunahpu and Xbalanque. You killed our father and our uncle. We are here to avenge their suffering."

The lords got down on the ground and cried out, "Take pity on us, Hunahpu and Xbalanque!"

"Very well. This is your sentence. From this day on, you will not be worshipped with sacrifices of blood and hearts. Instead you will be contented with the smoke of incense. Further, you will not attack innocent people. You will feed only on those who are weak, wicked, and worthless."

So it was that the rulers of Xibalba lost their power, and the earth became a safer place for humans. After their victory the boys returned to the place of sacrifice and spoke to the remains of One and Seven Hunahpu. They assured their father and uncle that their names would never be forgotten.

> THE TWO BOYS . . . ASCENDED STRAIGHT ON INTO THE SKY, AND THE SUN BELONGS TO ONE AND THE MOON TO THE OTHER.
> ⌐POPUL VUH

Then the Hero Twins rose from the underworld, straight up into the sky. One of them became the sun, and the other became the full moon. And it was light on the face of the earth, as the sun rose for the first time.

THE ANCIENT MAYA SPEAK
The BLESSING of the CORN

The myth of the Hero Twins explains the origins of a number of Maya customs, including an ancient harvest ritual. Before journeying to the underworld, Hunahpu and Xbalanque place ears of corn in the center of their grandmother's house. They tell Xmucane that the withering of the corn will be a sign of their death, while the sprouting of a new crop will signal their rebirth. In this passage from the *Popul Vuh*, the boys have died in the fiery pit of Xibalba, and the corn has dried out. Their grandmother burns copal (incense made from tree sap) in front of the ears, and they return to life. Today Quiché Maya farmers still pass a few ears of harvested corn through copal smoke. The dedicated ears are stored in the center of the family's attic until the new crop ripens in the field. The ritual is a reminder that, although the corn may wither, its life force never dies.

And this is their grandmother, crying and calling out in front of the corn ears they left planted. Corn plants grew, then dried up.

And this was when [the Hero Twins] were burned in the oven; then the corn plants grew again.

And this was when their grandmother burned something, she burned copal before the corn as a memorial to them. There was happiness in their grandmother's heart the second time the corn plants sprouted. Then the ears were deified [made holy] by their grandmother. . . . They had been left behind, planted by Hunahpu and Xbalanque, simply as a way for their grandmother to remember them.

Above: The descendants of the ancient Maya still celebrate the Fiesta del Maiz, or "Corn Festival."

THE ORIGINS *of the* QUICHÉ MAYA

The People of Corn

THE MYTH THAT CONCLUDES THE *POPUL VUH* TAKES US back in time once again. As the story begins, the Hero Twins have defeated the lords of Xibalba but have not yet risen into the sky. Although the world is still dark, the boy-gods' victories have made it a safer place for human habitation. This means that the creator gods Huracan and Gucumatz can return to the problem of making human beings. Their earlier efforts—the people made from mud and from wood—were failures. This time they use corn to make a new race of humans. The first four men they create will become the forefathers of the Quiché people.

As the Quiché multiply, they adopt Tohil as their special patron and protector. This ancient Maya god of fire was a form of the creator god Huracan. Under Tohil's guidance, the people begin a long migration to their promised homeland. During their journey, they witness the rising of Venus the morning star, followed by the first sunrise.

Opposite: According to Maya mythology, the first true people were made from corn.

This statue from the Maya city of Copán shows the corn god as a beautiful young man, with his hair forming the corn silk.

The story of the creation of the Quiché people highlights the importance of corn to the ancient Maya. Corn was the Maya's main food crop, essential to their survival. It was also a sacred symbol of life and an object of worship. It is not surprising that the creator gods chose to make the first true humans from this vital food.

The myth also explains the origins of a number of ancient Maya rituals and customs. Tohil is the source of the first fire, which he creates by spinning on his heel. The Maya made sparks for fire by spinning a stick called a fire drill against a wooden platform. In addition, Tohil is responsible for starting the practice of blood sacrifice. When a freezing storm hits, the god refuses to give fire to the people of other tribes until they agree to allow themselves to be "suckled." Unfortunately for the Maya's enemies, being "suckled" by Tohil meant having their sides cut open and their hearts offered in sacrifice.

CAST *of* CHARACTERS

Hunahpu (hoo-nah-POO)
Xbalanque (shbah-lahn-KAY) } The **Hero Twins**

Huracan (hoo-rah-KAHN) God of the sky and creation; also called **Heart of Sky**

Gucumatz (goo-koo-MAHTS) God of the sea and creation; also called the **Plumed Serpent**

Xmucane (shmoo-kah-NAY) Grandmother of the gods

Jaguar Quitze (keet-SAY)
Jaguar Night
Mahucutah (mah-hoo-koo-TAH)
True Jaguar } First humans; fathers of the Quiché people

Celebrated Seahorse
Prawn House
Hummingbird House
Macaw House } First women; mothers of the Quiché people

Tohil (toe-HEEL) Patron god of the Quiché; god of fire and storms

The Creation of Humans

THE HERO TWINS HAD DEFEATED the lords of death. It was nearly time for the sun, moon, and stars to appear. But still the creators had not found the right ingredients for humanity. Huracan, great god of the sky, and Gucumatz, the Plumed Serpent, spoke: "The time of dawn is approaching. Let us finish the work of making the people who will praise us and nurture us."

The gods talked and reflected. At last the answer became clear. With the help of the animals, they discovered what was needed to make the flesh and blood of humans.

These are the animals who showed them the way: the fox, coyote, parrot, and crow. The four animals brought news of a mountain called Broken Place, Bitter Water Place. This wonderful mountain was filled with yellow corn, white corn, and every other good food.

Heart of Sky and the Plumed Serpent followed the animals to the mountain. They were pleased when they saw its abundance. They took up the ears of yellow and white corn. Then they called for the wise grandmother Xmucane.

Xmucane ground the corn kernels into a fine meal. She rinsed her hands with clear water. Heart of Sky and the Plumed Serpent kneaded the cornmeal and water together. They shaped the dough into four humans. These are the names of the first fathers: Jaguar Quitze, Jaguar Night, Mahucutah, and True Jaguar.

The new humans were everything the gods had hoped for. They walked and they worked. They looked and they listened. They spoke in words and sang the praises of their creators:

Xmucane ground the corn into meal, just like a woman making tortillas.

We have been given
our mouths, our faces.
We speak, we hear,
we think, we walk.
We have seen what is great and small.
We understand what is far and near.
We give you thanks,
Our Creator and Maker!

When the gods heard the song, they were troubled. Perhaps their creations were *too* perfect. The humans could see everything in the world. They could stand in one place and observe all the trees, rocks, lakes, seas, and mountains. And with their perfect vision came perfect understanding.

"It is not right," said Heart of Sky and the Plumed Serpent. "Men should not become as great as the gods, who see and know everything. Let us take back just a little of their knowledge."

So Heart of Sky blew a fog over the eyes of the four humans. Their vision was dimmed, just as the face of a mirror becomes clouded when someone breathes upon it. Now the men could only see clearly what was nearby. They lost the means of seeing and knowing everything.

"Now let them multiply," said the creators. "Let humans flourish on the face of the earth." Then the gods created four truly beautiful women to become the wives of the first men. They made Celebrated Seahorse for Jaguar Quitze, Prawn House for Jaguar Night, Hummingbird House for Mahucutah, and Macaw House for True Jaguar.

It was as if the men had been asleep before these four women were created. With their wives by their sides, they became truly awake and happy. The women would go on to become great ladies. They would give birth to the people who would found all the houses, small and great. And together the first fathers and mothers were the root of the Quiché people.

The Great Migration

THE BIRTH OF THE QUICHÉ took place in a land far to the east. Other peoples came to this land, until there were many tribes, speaking many languages. In the midst of all these peoples, the Quiché remembered Heart of Sky and the Plumed Serpent. They fasted and prayed. They gave praise to the creators. They lifted their faces to the sky and asked the gods to send the light of morning. For the sun had not yet risen, and all the creatures of the earth still wandered about in the twilight.

In time the people grew weary of waiting for the dawn. They decided to go to the holy city of Tulan Zuyua. Countless people from many different tribes made the journey. When they arrived in the city, the gods were given out in order, one to each great house or tribe. Tohil, lord of fire, went to the leading Quiché families. Now the Quiché had a patron god to watch over them and a sacred image to honor with sacrifices.

It was cold at Tulan, before the rising of the sun. Tohil gave the people the gift of fire to keep them warm. One day a great hailstorm put out all the fires. The Quiché prayed to their god: "Help us, Tohil. We shall die of the cold."

"Do not worry," said Tohil. Then the god pivoted inside his sandal and started a fire.

The god of fire became the special protector of the Quiché people.

Now the Quiché were warm, but the people of the other tribes were freezing. Their arms and legs were shaking. Their teeth were chattering. Doubled over in pain, they presented themselves to Jaguar Quitze and the other lords. "Take pity on us," they said. "Let us have a little something from your fire."

"The fire belongs to Tohil. You must promise him something in return for his gift," said the Quiché lords.

"We will give him whatever he asks for," the tribes answered.

"When the time comes, you must embrace him. You must allow him to suckle you on your sides, under your arms."

"Very well," said the shivering people, and they received their fire.

Quiché warriors would raid enemy villages to capture prisoners for sacrifice.

They did not know that they were already defeated. In the days to come, the Quiché would subdue all the other tribes. Then the priests would cut open the people on their sides, under their arms, and offer their hearts to Tohil.

After the people had lived at Tulan for some time, Tohil spoke to the Quiché lords: "Our home is not here. Let us go on to the place where we belong."

So the people placed the image of Tohil in a wooden frame borne on the back of Jaguar Quitze. They gave thanks to their god with their blood, passing cords through their ears and elbows. Then they set forth on the difficult journey to their new homeland.

For many long days, the people wandered. They crossed over flooded plains, stepping on stones piled up in the sand. They passed the Great Abyss at the eastern edge of the earth. They turned west and entered the highlands. As they traveled, they kept watching for the morning star, which comes before the dawn.

In time the weary people reached a great mountain called Place of Advice. Jaguar Quitze, Jaguar Night, Mahucutah, and True Jaguar, together with their wives, waited on the mountaintop. They ate no food. They took no sleep or rest. They cried bitter tears, because they had led their people into exile and still they lived in darkness.

Then at last the people had their dawning. First came the morning star, and its face was brilliant. The people unwrapped the precious incense that they had carried all the way from Tulan. With joy in their hearts, they sent the smoke rising toward the great star.

Then they witnessed the birth of the sun. The first rising was unlike any other. The sun revealed himself as a person. His heat was almost unbearable. His face was so hot that it dried out the damp and muddy surface of the earth.

All the animals, small and great, cried out in joy as the darkness vanished. The puma and jaguar roared. The birds spread their wings and broke into song.

WHEN THE SUN HAD RISEN JUST A SHORT DISTANCE HE WAS LIKE A PERSON.
—POPUL VUH

On the top of the mountain, the Quiché people danced and burned their incense. In the midst of their joy, they remembered the people of other tribes, who witnessed the dawn in faraway places. There were countless tribes, scattered all over the land, but there was just one dawn for all the people.

In the years to come, the Quiché would move farther east, to their true homeland. There they would become a great nation, conquering many tribes and taking many people for sacrifice. The descendants of the first fathers would rule over the land in fiery splendor. For twelve generations the Quiché lords would rule, until the coming of the Spaniards.

GLOSSARY

calabash a large fruit or gourd whose hard shell is used to make bowls and other utensils

city-states independent states, each made up of a city and its surrounding territory

codices (KOE-duh-seez) early religious or historical texts. The Maya codices consisted of hieroglyphs and images painted on bark or deer hide, which was folded accordion style; the singular form is *codex*

culture heroes mythological heroes who help humankind through their acts of courage and discovery

deities gods, goddesses, and other divine beings

diviners people who practice the art of divining or divination; Maya diviners use methods including the casting of lots to communicate with the gods and spirits and discover hidden knowledge

hieroglyphs (HIE-ruh-glifs) an ancient writing system based on pictures and symbols that stand for words, sounds, and ideas

legend a traditional story that may involve ordinary mortals as well as divine beings and may be partly based on real people and events

macaw a type of parrot native to Mesoamerica; the scarlet macaw has brightly colored feathers that are mostly red

maize a tall variety of corn native to the Americas

Mesoamerica a cultural region that includes much of modern-day Mexico, Guatemala, and Belize, as well as parts of Honduras, El Salvador, Nicaragua, and Costa Rica; the ancient Maya occupied a large section of southern Mesoamerica

mythology the whole body of myths belonging to a people

myths traditional stories about gods and other divine beings, which were developed by ancient cultures to explain the mysteries of the physical and spiritual worlds

nance (NON-say) the small orange-yellow fruit of a tropical tree that grows from Mexico to South America

patron a god or goddess who was believed to be the special protector of a group of people

Pleiades (PLEE-uh-deez) a bright cluster of stars in the constellation Taurus; the Quiché name for the Pleiades is Motz

quetzal (ket-SAHL) a Central American bird with bright green feathers

tricksters mythological characters who serve as comical mischief makers, defeating their enemies through their cleverness and trickery; tricksters can also be powerful culture heroes

Xibalba (she-bahl-BAH) the Maya underworld; the name means "Place of Fright"

ABOUT *the* POPUL VUH

The *Popul Vuh*, or "Council Book," was the most important sacred text of the Quiché, the Maya people who built a great kingdom in the highlands of Guatemala. This ancient codex covered a broad sweep of mythical history. It reached all the way from the gods' creation of the world and humans through the great migration of the Quiché people and the deeds of their early rulers. When the lords of Quiché sat in council, they consulted the *Popul Vuh* in order to peer into the past and draw on the wisdom of their gods and ancestors.

Like all Maya, the Quiché were skilled astronomers who looked to the heavens for inspiration and guidance. The original creators of the *Popul Vuh* built their text on the movements of the heavenly bodies. The divine characters in the book's myths—including One and Seven Hunahpu,

A clay figure of a Maya astronomer-priest

Blood Woman, and the Hero Twins—move in and out of the under-world realm of Xibalba. Their movements are linked with the cycles of the sun, moon, stars, and planets. For example, the descent of One and Seven Hunahpu to the underworld corresponds to the time when Venus dips below the eastern horizon. When One Hunahpu is killed, his head is placed in a tree, representing the reappearance of Venus as the evening star.

After the Spanish conquered the Quiché in 1524, they destroyed all known copies of the *Popul Vuh*. Sometime in the 1550s, an anony-mous group of Quiché nobles secretly reconstructed the ancient text. The nobles probably worked from their memories of oral per-formances of the *Popul Vuh*. Instead of using the hieroglyphics of the original codex, they wrote in an alphabetic spelling system that had been developed by Spanish priests. Through their efforts, a form of writing created for the publishing of Christian literature in Maya lan-guages helped preserve the people's ancient religious beliefs for future generations.

Around 1700 a young Spanish priest named Francisco Ximénez came across a copy of the nobles' manuscript. By that time, Spain's fervor for stamping out the ancient religions of Mesoamerica had faded. Ximénez made a copy of the text and also translated it into Spanish. The Quiché manuscript later disappeared, but the priest's copy survived. The *Popul Vuh* has since been translated into a number of languages, including French, German, English, and Japanese. Today it is regarded as the most complete source of the ancient myths not only of the Maya but of any Mesoamerican people.

To FIND OUT MORE

BOOKS

Dalal, Anita. *Myths of Pre-Columbian America.* Austin, TX: Raintree Steck-Vaughn, 2001.

Faiella, Graham. *Mesoamerican Mythology.* New York: Rosen, 2006.

Jones, David M. *Mythology of the Aztecs and Maya.* London: Southwater, 2003.

Laughton, Timothy. *The Maya: Life, Myth, and Art.* New York: Barnes and Noble Books, 2004.

Menchú, Rigoberta, and Dante Liano. *The Honey Jar.* Translated by David Unger. Toronto, Canada: Groundwood Books, 2006.

Perl, Lila. *The Ancient Maya.* New York: Scholastic, 2005.

Schuman, Michael A. *Mayan and Aztec Mythology.* Berkeley Heights, NJ: Enslow, 2001.

West, David. *Mesoamerican Myths.* Graphic Mythology series. New York: Rosen, 2006.

WEB SITES

The Big Myth at http://www.mythicjourneys.org/bigmyth
   The Big Myth uses narration and flash animation to tell the creation stories of twenty-five cultures, including the Maya. You'll need to download Shockwave to view this entertaining site, which was developed for use in primary schools in Europe.

Encyclopedia Mythica: Maya Mythology at
   http://www.pantheon.org/areas/mythology/americas/maya
   This online encyclopedia offers more than 125 brief articles on Maya gods, goddesses, giants, demons, and other mythological beings.

The Gods of Mayan Mythology at
   http://www.godchecker.com/pantheon/mayan-mythology.php
   Godchecker is an online encyclopedia with a great sense of humor. The site includes a brief introduction to Maya mythology plus lively articles on more than one hundred gods and goddesses.

Internet Sacred Text Archive: Popul Vuh at
    http://www.sacred-texts.com/nam/maya/index.htm
    The *Internet Sacred Text Archive* is an online library of texts on
    religion, mythology, and related topics, which have been scanned
    from the original books and articles. The site includes several
    texts by and about the Maya.

Mayan Kids at http://www.mayankids.com/mkintro.htm
    This colorful site offers information on a wide variety of topics
    related to Maya history, culture, daily life, and beliefs. Nice
    features include a glossary, clip art, and an assortment of
    interactive games.

SELECTED BIBLIOGRAPHY

Allan, Tony. *Gods of Sun and Sacrifice: Aztec and Maya Myth.* London:
    Duncan Baird, 1997.
Ferguson, Diana. *Tales of the Plumed Serpent: Aztec, Inca and Mayan Myths.*
    London: Collins and Brown, 2000.
Foster, Lynn V. *Handbook to Life in the Ancient Maya World.* New York:
    Facts on File, 2002.
León-Portilla, Miguel. *Pre-Columbian Literatures of Mexico.* Norman,
    OK: University of Oklahoma Press, 1969.
Markman, Roberta H., and Peter T. Markman. *The Flayed God:
    Mesoamerican Mythological Tradition.* San Francisco, CA: Harper
    San Francisco, 1992.
Nicholson, Irene. *Mexican and Central American Mythology.* New York: Peter
    Bedrick, 1987.
Phillips, Charles. *The Aztec and Maya World.* London: Lorenz Books,
    2005.
————. *The Mythology of the Aztec and Maya.* London: Southwater,
    2006.

Read, Kay Almere, and Jason J. González. *Handbook of Mesoamerican Mythology*. Santa Barbara, CA: ABC-CLIO, 2000.

Roberts, Timothy R. *Gods of the Maya, Aztecs, and Incas*. New York: MetroBooks, 1996.

Sharer, Robert J. *Daily Life in Maya Civilization*. Westport, CT: Greenwood Press, 1996.

Taube, Karl. *Aztec and Maya Myths*. Austin: University of Texas Press, 1993.

Tedlock, Dennis, trans. *Popul Vuh*. New York: Simon and Schuster, 1985.

NOTES *on* QUOTATIONS

Quoted passages in sidebars come from the following sources:

"The Light of History," page 38, from *The Book of the People: Popul Vuh*, translated by Delia Goetz and Sylvanus Griswold Morley (Los Angeles: Plantin Press, 1954) at http://www.sacred-texts.com/nam/maya/pvgm/pv08.htm, and from *Popul Vuh*, translated by Dennis Tedlock (New York: Simon and Schuster, 1985).

"The Four Hundred Boys," page 55, and "The Blessing of the Corn," page 77, from *Popul Vuh*, translated by Dennis Tedlock (New York: Simon and Schuster, 1985).

Above: One of the few surviving Maya codices, or screenfold books

INDEX

ABOUT *the* AUTHOR

"I can't think of a better way to learn about the people of ancient cultures than by reading the stories that held their deepest hopes and fears, their most cherished values and beliefs. While collecting these sacred tales, I looked for the elements that set each culture apart: the special music of the language, the differing roles of men and women, the unique ways of interpreting the mysteries of life. I also enjoyed discovering the many feelings and experiences that unite all peoples around the world, both past and present. Pueblo storyteller Harold Littlebird said it best: 'We know we all come from story. They may not all be the same story but there is a sameness. There is a oneness in it all.' "

VIRGINIA SCHOMP has written more than seventy titles for young readers on topics including dinosaurs, dolphins, occupations, American history, and ancient cultures. Ms. Schomp earned a Bachelor of Arts degree in English Literature from Penn State University. She lives in the Catskill Mountain region of New York with her husband, Richard, and their son, Chip.